EMPTYING OUT THE NEGATIVITY

DANARIO LANKFORD

Step 1: Emptying Out The Negativity {page 10}
Chapter 1 Empowerment {page 25}
Chapter 2 Encouragement {page 37}
Chapter 3 Plan To Succeed {page 43}
Chapter 4 Have Faith And Believe {page 49}
Chapter 5 Speak Kind Words {page 57}
Chapter 6 Positive Advice {{page 70}
About Author {page 87}

All rights reserved. No part of this book may be reproduced, stored in a retrieval system, or transmitted in any form without written permission from the author, except by the reviewers who may quote brief excerpts in connection with a review. For information regarding please write to: Danario Lankford
Danario.lank@gmail.com

A Book filled with Positive Affirmations and Tips for living a Positive lifestyle

By Danario Lankford

Prologue

When someone gives us flowers, the most common thing is to place the flowers in a vase containing water. Over time, the water becomes stagnant, appearing cloudy, and it may even begin to smell. When this begins to happen, things have to change-you must empty out the old water and replace the vase with new water. The point is when something is being emptied, there will come a time when it will require a refill.

This book is called Emptying Out the Negativity. Once you've emptied out the negative and toxic things in your life, what will you fill yourself back up with?

Will it be positive or negative? Think of it this way, after removing that murky water from the vase of flowers, are you really going to replace it with more unclean water?

I need you to know that change does not happen overnight; however, to begin the change, it does require you to move-taking one step at a time.

So, welcome!

God Bless You, and I hope you enjoy the book.

Let's Go!

Step 1: Emptying Out the Negativity

I feel we as individuals should leave no room for the negative. We must learn to respond to it in a proper way and not let the negative overtake us.

The first step to emptying the negative and toxic things in your life is acknowledging it. Acknowledge the problem at hand. I say this because no one knows you better than you know yourself. Be honest with yourself and start working towards positive solutions for a positive change.

Changing the mindset is very important. Our minds are very powerful tools and assets that can work for our good. Like the saying goes, "Don't let your mind go to waste."

Let's Get It!

Let's Get It!

Let's Get It!

12

While doing some research, I learned about common negative thought patterns people can have and realized I was guilty of some too. I saw a couple of my thought patterns as well. Man, change *is* and *will* come.

Some common negative thoughts can be:

> Life moves so fast! I cannot keep up.
>
> Life is frantic and uncontrollable.
>
> I have too much to do.

I'm not worthy of my success.

The world is an awful place.

Everyone is awful except me.

I'm a failure.

I quit. I'm done. I'm not doing it.

They don't like me.

I should be more like 'that' person.

They're rich, why aren't I?

STOP IT...STOP IT...STOP IT

Now, if you've seen at least one of your thoughts up top, put an 'X' by each thought. If you feel you have some of your own, that you don't see listed above-write them down. You just might be surprised at what you'll see.

MENTAL HEALTH

Now, if you are in a bad
mood, just meditate by
meditating. Because
thoughts. If you feel you
have some of your own
that you don't care listed
above, write them down.
You just might be surprised
at what you find.

Time to be transparent. Who are you trying to impress? And, if you have this kind of thinking...please remove it.

I'm not saying you're a bad person or that you are wrong for what you think, but you must learn not to let the negative thoughts sink in and grow. It can become very toxic in your life.

I like to tell people, "life is not a sprint; it's a marathon." You must learn to work at your own pace. Focus on improving yourself, taking care of your responsibilities and priorities, accomplishing your goals, and bringing your dreams to reality.

Understand, we are all human beings on this earth, and everything is not always going to be 'peaches and cream' (when everything seems perfect and fine).

There will be good days and bad days. We all have them. Yet, let us not allow the negative or bad circumstances to control or dictate our now and future.

My whole concept of creating this book is to help change the thinking process from a negative, poverty-stricken mentality to a positive and productive mindset.

Understand, you are in control of your destiny and success in life. It all comes down to the decisions and choices we make in life.

Two things I've come to realize and understand in life is: we cannot change everything, and it does not stay dark all the time.

There has to come sunshine.

NOW ASK YOURSELF

What do I want in life?

How can I achieve it?

What do I need to improve and develop myself?

Where do I want to go in life?

Do I want to become successful?

Do I want to become wealthy?

Do I want to take care of my children and family?

Do I want to graduate?

Do I want to get a trade, job, career, or start the business I've always thought about?

Know that all things are possible. But it's all up to you. Believe! Believe that you can achieve. Believe! Believe that you can do it. Believe! Believe that it can happen.

You are a diamond created to do great things in life. Remember, there is purpose in you. You were created with greatness.

Now, before you turn to the next page, clear your mind, and let's go get it!

Let's start by removing the negativity.

Remember, life's a process, and nothing happens overnight. As you've just read previously, acknowledging that life's not a sprint: it is a marathon. It's about taking steps and building towards a better and greater you.

You can do it.

1

Empowerment

At times, life can be difficult and frustrating. However, I want to say to you; YOU CAN OVERCOME! Don't quit. Don't give up. Be strong and stand tall.

I had to understand that I could not change nor control everything that happens in life. However, I do have the power to control the choices and decisions I make in my life. It's called a 'belief system' which basically means believing that you can accomplish great things in life.

All you have to do is BELIEVE you can do it!

Empowerment is about exercising the power and authority already built within you. This power and authority are released by executing strength and confidence in whatever you do in life.

When I learned I was a provider and had people depending on me, I had to step my game up. If there was procrastination in me, it was not going to win. If you want something... set some goals towards it and *go, get it!*

Affirmations of Empowerment

Affirmations are primarily a way to practice positive thinking and self-empowerment. They can be simple, positive statements that declare specific goals.

These empowering words, when repeated throughout your day, can have intense effects on the conscious and unconscious mind.

Having daily affirmations will give you a positive mental attitude that will help you achieve success in almost anything.

Affirmations have helped a lot of people make changes in their lives and, for others, have done nothing at all. Reason is because not everyone wants it. You have to be receptive to the program.

Affirmations can have the ability to program your mind into believing the concept. So how do you program your mind?

You have to want change for change to happen and by reading this book, it looks like you're on the right path.

Let's get started!

Before you begin, try to clear your heart and mind by taking some deep breaths, slowly inhaling and exhaling to a count of three.

Look yourself in the eye by standing in front of a mirror and say your affirmations with confidence, slowly and clearly. Allowing yourself to only hear you. Focus on the meaning of each word of statement by repeating it 3 to 5 times.

You should also practice affirming yourself throughout the day to maintain this way of thinking.

This chapter will conclude with some of my own self-affirmations that have helped me slowly transform my life.

Also, take notice of how my last two affirmations are repeated. They're emphasized because that is what I wanted most in life.

Self-Affirmations

- ◊ I believe I will achieve.
- ◊ I am a champion.
- ◊ I am great.
- ◊ I am more than a conqueror.
- ◊ I am a child of God.
- ◊ I am strong.
- ◊ I am a winner.
- ◊ I am wealthy.
- ◊ I am successful.
- ◊ I am valuable.
- ◊ I am more than enough.

- ◊ I am committed.
- ◊ I am dedicated.
- ◊ I will do great things in life.
- ◊ I can and will succeed in life.
- ◊ I am determined.
- ◊ I will work towards my goals and make accomplishments.
- ◊ I refuse to fail.
- ◊ I will work towards a better me.
- ◊ **I will do great things in life.**
- ◊ **I can and will succeed in life.**

Now it's your turn. Write down ten affirmations for your life and begin your daily life-changing transition. Feel free to use the above affirmations that have helped change my life.

1.

2.

3.

4.

5.

6.

7.

8.

9.

10.

35

Notes:

2

Encouragement

Looking at the word encouragement, you will find the word 'courage' which means, "the ability to face danger and deal with it." Encouragement is a great motivator. It helps to make people succeed and to accomplish their objectives.

Staying positive allows you to do whatever it is that you wish to accomplish with confidence. Set some goals, build a plan, and take action. Remember, greatness doesn't just happen. It's a process. You must work at it! Put in the effort and work at it. You can do it!

<u>Affirmations of Encouragement</u>

- ◊ In the roughest times, I will learn to persevere and press forward. I will not fold or quit.
- ◊ Winners will always win because winners don't quit.
- ◊ Giving up is not an option. Winning is.

- ◊ I stand for something because I don't fall for anything.
- ◊ I stand on morals, values, and principles.
- ◊ Even though challenges will come in my life, I will not give up the fight. I will stand strong and fight with powerful might.
- ◊ Positivity will always outlast the negative.

- ◊ Consistency is key in accomplishing your goals.
- ◊ If it's hard, it just means I'll need to have faith and go harder. Nothing great was ever achieved without effort and enthusiasm.
- ◊ I am love. I am purpose.
- ◊ I am in charge of how I feel, and today, I'm choosing happiness.

Now it's your turn to take a step of faith and create some of your own encouragement for yourself or for someone else.

3

Plan to Succeed

When you succeed, you've achieved something that you have been aiming for or have gained the desired results in which you were seeking.

It is better to have a plan than to have no plan at all. Start by setting some goals.

Setting goals and creating a plan can serve a great purpose that could potentially help you through life.

Sometimes life will make you feel as though you're on a road trip. Having a plan is like having a road map. It will give you directions towards your goals, rewards, and accomplishments you'll set forth in life.

It is your navigation system. Without it, you could end up lost or simply going around in circles.

The following page gives you affirmations to inspire you to succeed. Remember, it's all up to you.

Affirmations to Succeed

- ◊ Plans are a road map to my rewards.
- ◊ Plans are like a GPS system; they give me direction to achieve my goals.
- ◊ A plan is better than no plan at all.
- ◊ I plan to succeed, not fail.
- ◊ A dream with action can come true.
- ◊ A dream without action is just imagination.

- ◊ I dream big with no limitations.
- ◊ I believe my dreams will come true if I put in the effort and consistency.
- ◊ I am a successor. Success is mine.
- ◊ If it doesn't work the first time, try again. Don't quit, especially if it's worth anything.
- ◊ If I cannot find a lane, I will create my own.
- ◊ Consistency is a key to success. Use it.

On the following page, create some affirmations to succeed on your own. Think, plan and prepare to design a road map of your next destination. Let your journey begin!

4

Have Faith and Believe

Having faith to me, is dope! It's a confidence builder, an energy pusher.

To have faith will strengthen you, and it can be very exciting!

Faith gives you confidence in the unknown. It is a critical component in life.

Without it, it's almost impossible to achieve goals, love others, or take on the realities that you are an achiever and you can succeed.

Belief is the power that lies in its ability to create vision, strength of will, and resilience.

Belief ignites and activates, even if it's something that you can't touch or see at that moment.

When you're able to maintain a deep belief and keep strong hope in whatever situation or circumstance life throws at you, that becomes a reward in itself.

When you look at it, faith is like planting a seed in the ground.

Once planted, you're unable to see the beginning stages of development, and you have no idea if the seed will grow.

You believe and have hope that the seed will grow into a plant; therefore, you will continue to water and tend to it.

This is very similar to what we go through in life. We have dreams and goals that we can neither see nor touch at that time; however, we still must work at it in hopes that the dream comes true.

On the next page is some affirmations to remember. These are the positive things you should fill your mind with as you release the negative.

Affirmations of Faith and Belief

All things are possible with God.

I am Awesome.

I have all the strength and confidence within me that I need to succeed.

I am in control of my life.

Today will be a good day.

Even though I cannot see the things I am in expectation of, I will continue to work towards what I believe in.

"Faith is the substance of things hoped for and the evidence of things not seen." Hebrews 1:1

I *will* work each day towards improving myself to become a better version of myself.

Greatness just doesn't happen overnight. It takes focus and effort every day.

If I think and believe it, I can achieve it.

I have control over my thoughts.

I believe I can do anything.

****

What is it you have faith in? What is your belief?

The next page is your dreams, your goals, and your wishes. Go and be great!

God teach me how to love unselfishly. Faith and hope can go a long way. If no one else believes, I still won't stop believing.

Your Notes:

5

Speak Kind Words

"A soft answer turns away wrath, but a harsh word stirs up anger." -Proverbs 15:1

Words are very powerful. When you speak words of kindness to someone, it can really have an impact on their life.

Speaking kind words can uplift, motivate and encourage someone. These simple words can bring joy and brightness to a person's day.

Kind words can also heal and help strengthen someone who can't find the strength within themselves.

These words have the capability to fill a person with positivity. It will also make the speaker a happier and more inspiring person.

In addition to creating an emotional impact, kind words are also able to make a difference within our thinking and our response to situations.

Kind words should be spoken sincerely and with compassion because they are coming from the heart.

Therefore, we consider speaking kind words an art form. It takes practice and mistakes to know what is best for the particular moment.

However, do not be afraid to have the courage to speak out, and please do not forget, one kind word can go a long way.

Affirmations of Kind Words

Kind words do not cost anything. Yet, they accomplish a lot.

I speak with kindness.

One small kind deed can change an entire day.

Loving and kind words are very powerful and uplifting.

One kind word can help bring change in a person's life for the better.

Kind words come with peace.

"Gracious words are like a honeycomb,

Sweetness to the soul and health to the body"- Proverbs 16:24

Encourage and build one another up.

Kind words are melodies of the heart.

How did this chapter make you feel?

Did it make you feel like going out and making an impact on someone today, or perhaps yourself?

Don't worry if it didn't. Remember, this is a process, and processes can take time.

Keep at it! Keep affirming! You will get there.

Use the next page to master the art of speaking kind words by writing down a few of your own to spread some joy.

■ ■

Now that you have an idea of how to remove the negativity and replace it with positivity. Let's look at some positive advice tips.

These positive tips will help build towards a more positive lifestyle. Think about what you prefer; a positive lifestyle or a negative one?

Being positive always exceeds the negative-it is healthy for the mind, body, and soul.

Being positive can be energy driven, uplifting,

helpful, productive, hopeful, effective, and cheerful. Understand in life, there may be moments of sadness, failures, and obstacles that will need to be acknowledged.

Never give it too much of your time. Instead, view them as lessons and strive to find ways and tools to overcome them.

Not everyone will get it right the first or second time. That does not mean give up.

I'm here to tell you:
NEVER QUIT ON YOUR DREAMS AND GOALS-

They contain purpose!

Remember, no one is perfect. It can take hard work to become a better version of ourselves, and we all can use a little improving.

Even some of our leaders could use some improving of their own. No one is perfect.

Moving on... Let's Build! Let us build towards a

better attitude within our character.

Now ask yourself these questions:

- How can I improve?
- How can I do better?
- What do I need to self-reflect on?
- What is my self-evaluation?

Think about the questions you've just asked yourself and use the following page to write your answers.

Being true to yourself allows space for change to enter.

6

Positive Advice Tips

I. When you are facing a problem, focus on solutions. Refuse to allow your mind to wander around difficult and negative results. Instead, think of the positive solution to come.
II. Acknowledge your problems and difficulties but face them with courage

and a positive attitude.

III. Smile more often when in the company of others. It brings joy and will brighten up the scene.

IV. Kindness and being friendly are peaceful and warm.

V. Learn to let go. You'll waste a lot of time and energy attaching yourself to things, habits, or people of the past. None are useful.

VI. If you are bothered by something, hurt

by someone, or just simply disturbed in your life, learn to detach from it emotionally. This helps protect you from unwanted anxiety, drama, or stress.

VII. Don't be afraid to show courage, self-esteem, and assertiveness while counting to be kind and tolerant towards someone.

VIII. Eat healthily. Eat less junk food.

IX. Exercise your body regularly. Taking

walks will relieve tension.
X. Strive to be more positive and optimistic.
XI. Don't allow yourself to get wrapped in fears, worry, or criticism of others. Look for ways to improve your life and your lifestyle.
XII. When solving your problems, try to remain jovial (cheerful/friendly) while you strive for better.

XIII. Choose happiness and focus on happiness.
XIV. Get out of your comfort zone. Don't be afraid of the new and unfamiliar.
XV. Resist the temptation of procrastination. It is not your friend.
XVI. Don't rush, but get things done in a timely and orderly fashion.
XVII. Always be willing to improve and develop yourself through life.

	Practice makes perfect.
XVIII.	Believe in yourself and never count yourself out.
XIX.	No one in life is perfect.
XX.	Be consistent in whatever you do. Take it one day at a time, but never overwhelm yourself.
XXI.	Finding balance and time management is important to learn in life.
XXII.	Strive to change your mindset

towards life with a little effort and perseverance.
XXIII. Think positive and push for better. You can do it!
XXIV. Your time, your mind, your ideas, and your creativity are an asset in your life.
XXV. You are valuable, and you are somebody. Never settle for mediocre because you have greatness inside of you.

I can honestly say, if you've made it this far, you're on your way to something better, something greater!

Continue to believe. Have hope and stay persistent in life. Don't ever quit! ...Now that's a Champion/Winner mentality.

In conclusion, small steps do equal a greater distance. Let's look at the definition of Self-Improvement.

Self-improvement *is the act or process of improving oneself by one's own action* .

When dealing with change, it doesn't happen overnight. But what can happen is, small steps can lead to a greater distance. Take it one day at a time and allow the results to stack up.

Through my own experiences in life, I learned that taking one or two steps towards a new way of life was more inspiring than not trying or attempting to move forward towards my self-improving. Just do nothing at all?... how could I, if I wanted to self-improve?

Firmly understand this: You have the legitimate right to be all you can be. You have the right to be successful and live life abundantly.

You were created and filled with joy, peace, wealth, love, faith, confidence, and creativity.

Life is what you make of it. As many know, life will

come with obstacles and challenges. However, you must remain consistent about being persistent to overcome and rise above the compounds. This is a reward within itself.

I've always said, *if you believe, then you can achieve it.* Do not let guilt, resentment, fear, doubt, or worry interfere. Remove those negative emotions. But how?

Most of us will 'blow' things out of proportion by replaying them in our minds time and time again.

Doing this, will not remove any negative emotions. It will only add to the problems and perhaps make matters worse.

We should also try and be reasonably willing to accept that bad feelings or negative thoughts are occasionally unavoidable.

When this occurs, we MUST think of ways to make ourselves 'feel better.' Also known as Self-care.

Taking time to relax or use calming activities are all a part of self-care. Reading, writing, and going for walks can also be great ways to distract your mind from the negative. Even talking with a close friend or family member can make you feel better.

Now that you have an idea of what could be done to rid the negativity, let's change the narrative.

****

Let's start looking at things on the positive side. No matter what 'We' as individuals go through in life, it will never change the fact that YOU are somebody. YOU are valuable, and YOU are more than enough.

You were created to do great things. Never let obstacles and difficulties stop you from living the best of life. Pain doesn't last forever... there has to be sunshine.

Smile a little more for a change, and go be the best you can be.

Another two things I've realized the past is the past, and no one can get time back.

Now you ask yourself *How do I want to live the rest of my life from this point forward?*

Let your now and future be filled with love, joy, peace, faith, and success!

Sincerely,

Danario Lankford

Press 4 Success and make your next move your best move.

P.S. God Bless and Go Be Your Best

ABOUT THE AUTHOR

Having shown fortitude in the face of a hostile society, Danario Lankford now lives with purpose.

He knows that he was destined to help encourage and inspire others through his life stories of overcoming obstacles and hardships. Danario was compelled to forfeit his youth at a young age. Having never seen his father and the second oldest of five siblings, Danario was raised in an unstructured, single-parent home where violence, abuse, and drugs were an everyday occurrence in his environment. By the age of twelve, Danario had dropped out of school and entered himself into a lifestyle of promiscuity, abuse of alcohol, marijuana, and selling illegal drugs. Which in turn, introduced him into the California Jail systems throughout his adolescent years.

When Danario came close to losing his life in 2017 due to gun violence, he acknowledged his life needed transformation but could not execute the change because guns and drug sales were still a part of his life. For months after, he struggled with forgiveness and wanted retaliation because of all the anger and pain he'd endured over the years. It wasn't until Danario accepted Christ into his life, when his transformation began. In strengthening his relationship with God, Danario's perspective began to change. He's now gained a passion to live better and wants to encourage and introduce this positive lifestyle to others, primarily addressing the youth. His outreach has led him to different organizations, including San Francisco

Juvenile Hall and various Bay Area high schools. Currently, Danario is active in the community and continues to motivate and inspire people. His primary goal is to create his own organization to provide the knowledge of empowering change.

Made in the USA
Middletown, DE
27 November 2024